TANDREKA DAVIS

Copyright ©2025 Tandreka Davis
When Loyalty Hurts

Paperback ISBN: 979-8-218-70765-1

Published by:
CoolBird Publishing House
2036 Cherokee Rd., Ste 38
Alexander City, AL 35010
www.coolbirdstudios.com

Book cover design: Taminko J. Kelley

All rights reserved. No part of this publication may be reproduced, stored in a retrieval system, or transmitted in any form by any means - electronic, mechanical, digital, photocopy, recording, or otherwise-without prior written permission of the author. Please purchase only authorized editions. References have been included in the back of this publication.

Printed in the United States of America

Disclaimer:

This book is a true account of the author's personal experiences. The events described herein are factual to the best of the author's knowledge and recollection. While the situations and emotions conveyed are real, the names and identifying details of individuals have been omitted to protect their privacy. The intent of this work is not to defame, malign, or harm any individual or group, but to share the author's truth, healing journey, and perspective on events that shaped her life. Any resemblance to actual persons, living or dead, is purely coincidental.

Dedication

To every woman who has ever been betrayed, humiliated, or made to feel less than her true worth: I stand before you as living proof that your ending can be profoundly beautiful. Remember that you possess an inner strength greater than those who have tried to break you. Stand tall and proud in your journey while healing on your own terms. Embrace every scar as a testament to your resilience.

CONTENTS

Chp 1 Loyalty and Trust Always Start Fresh...................9

Chp 2 Cut Them Both Off If You Have To.................14

Chp 3 Counterfeit Relationships...................................19

Chp 4 Betrayal of the Heart..25

Chp 5 My Friend & My Man..31

Chp 6 Healing Is A Process..43

Chp 7 The Wedding..55

Chp 8 My Turn On Paper...68

Chp 9 Moving from the Reality of It All.....................74

Chp 10 Meeting in the Courtroom................................81

Chp 11 The Move Forward..86

Chp 12 The Days Ahead..99

About the Author..124

Journal Your Thoughts...125

Introduction

Just as I am about to do in my book, when you feel ready, share your story with the world and let it resonate deeply; make those who hurt you pay attention from the front row. You may have faced the losses of relationships, financial stability, or even a sense of self but know this: your happy ending is still within reach. Do not settle for mere survival; rise from the ashes of your past, stronger and fiercer than ever before. The life you are stepping into is one that surpasses anything you have ever known.

Always remember that you are not alone in your struggle. Together, we will amplify our voices, break the silence, and reclaim our power. Let this be a call for all women to know that your story matters. Your healing matters, and your happiness is not just possible...it is inevitable. This is my story, "When Loyalty Hurts." May it inspire you to embrace your journey and celebrate the beauty that lies ahead of you. No matter what obstacle you face on the way to success.

-Tandreka

TANDREKA DAVIS

Chapter 1
Loyalty and Trust Always Start Fresh

In a whirlwind of passion and devotion, I found myself immersed in a four-year relationship with a man I adored deeply. Together, we forged a tapestry of countless memories and experiences that wove our lives together in a way that felt unbreakable. It was a love that promised forever, filled with laughter, shared dreams, and intimate moments that seemed to define our existence.

Before we decided to be in a relationship, he pursued me relentlessly for a year and a half and was determined to gain my attention and affection. His persistence was admirable yet overwhelming at times. Each day brought a new attempt, a new gesture crafted to win me over, but I remained hesitant. Then one fateful day, in a move that showcased both his creativity and determination, he sent his friend to ask for my number. Initially, I said no, standing firm in my resolve. However, his friend, sensing the opportunity, implored me to reconsider. He promised that my compliance would come with a reward because his friend was willing to pay him for successfully securing my number or coaxing me into calling him. Faced with such an unusual situation and tempted by the thrill of the moment, I finally gave in and called him, setting in motion the beautiful journey that would unfold between us.

Alongside him, I cultivated what I believed were genuine friendships and bonds that had stood the test of time, each one a thread in my life's fabric, intertwined with loyalty and understanding. Among these cherished connections, I welcomed a new companion into my inner circle: another woman, who quickly became an inseparable part of my life. From the moment we met, it felt like a cosmic alignment, as if the universe had conspired to unite our spirits. Together, we embarked on countless trips, exploring new states and savoring the thrill of adventure. Each journey strengthened our bond, as we created memories filled with laughter and discovery. Additionally, we ventured into business together, intertwining our dreams and aspirations in a shared pursuit. This partnership not only enriched our lives but also deepened the trust and loyalty we held for one another.

Our bond was electric, a connection that transcended the usual boundaries of friendship. In just three short years, we built a world of shared secrets, laughter, and dreams. It was as if we had known each other for a lifetime, sharing not only our joys but also our vulnerabilities. We became each other's confidantes, navigating the complexities of life together, and reveling in this newfound closeness.

Yet, beneath the surface of this seemingly idyllic existence lurked the shadows of betrayal and disloyalty, waiting to unravel the tightly knit tapestry of our lives. As I cherished these connections, little did I know that the very foundations of my relationships were on the brink of being collapsed, setting the stage for a heart-wrenching journey into the depths of disloyalty, betrayal and fake love.

"You're either loyal completely,
or not loyal at all."

– Sharnay

Chapter 2

Cut Them Both Off If You Have To

Initially, the bond I formed with my new companion felt like a breath of fresh air, a vibrant addition to my inner circle. Our friendship was a tapestry woven with laughter, deep conversations, and the intimate sharing of relationship woes. We became each other's unwavering support, navigating the highs and lows of life side by side. It seemed as if our souls resonated on the same frequency, creating an unshakeable connection that was invigorating.

But as time passed, something began to shift in the fabric of our friendship. Gradually, it became strangely apparent that we were no longer seeing eye to eye. The very spark that once ignited our conversations dimmed, giving way to an undercurrent of tension that

When Loyalty Hurts

I couldn't ignore. My intuition, that quiet yet powerful voice deep within, kept whispering that something was wrong and that perhaps she wasn't the friend I thought she was.

One day, I went to get my hair done by our shared hairdresser. This particular time, I went by myself, and the hairdresser had a lot to tell me. As I sat there getting my hair done, he brought up my friend's name and shared everything she had said and I mean things I had no clue about. So, being the woman that I am, I chose not to address my friend directly. Instead, I discerned what was true and what wasn't, and decided to cut both of them off...the hairdresser and my friend ...without another word.

One moment we were inseparable, sharing in each other's triumphs and tribulations; the next, we found ourselves at odds. How is it possible for grown women to drift apart so abruptly? It was as if a veil had been pulled back, exposing rifts that had been silently growing, but I was determined to understand what was lying beneath the surface.

I couldn't believe how the laughter that once filled our interactions began to fade and was replaced by awkward silences and misunderstandings; things grown women just shouldn't be doing. Our conversations that once flowed effortlessly became stilted and riddled with unspoken words and unresolved feelings. Have you ever experienced this? It was disheartening, to say the least. I often found myself pondering how two people who had once shared so much could now stand worlds apart.

As I wrestled with my feelings of confusion and betrayal, I couldn't help but reflect on the moments that had brought us together. Was it all an illusion? Had I been blind to the signs all along? My heart yearned for resolution, to mend the unraveling threads of our connection, yet deep down, I felt an unsettling pull urging me to tread carefully. But my loyalty was putting me in a dangerous position because not everyone's loyalty is the same, and I had to learn that the hard way.

"Disloyalty is not just a character flaw...it's a choice wrapped in selfish intent."

-Author Unknown

Chapter 3
Counterfeit Relationships

This chapter of loyalty, once marked by warmth and understanding, was now steeped in uncertainty. The path forward loomed ahead, shrouded in questions and doubt. Would I confront the issues head-on, risking the remnants of our friendship, or would I allow the currents of change to dictate the outcome? Each choice felt heavy with consequence, and I found myself grappling with the weight of my decisions. The memories of laughter and late-night conversations echoed in my mind, stark reminders of a bond that felt irrevocably altered.

One thing was clear: the journey ahead would force me to confront not only the complexities of our relationship but also the deeper truths about trust and loyalty that would ultimately shape my story. I knew

When Loyalty Hurts

that this experience could either lead to a painful reckoning or an opportunity for growth. As I stood at this crossroad, I realized that it wasn't just about salvaging a friendship; it was about discovering the strength within myself to navigate the murky waters of betrayal and allegiance. The lessons learned in this crucible would be invaluable, guiding me as I sought to redefine what loyalty truly meant in my life.

Truthfully, I found myself grappling with the confusion of our fallout. It felt surreal, like a scene pulled from a twisted dream. As I reflected on the events that unfolded, a troubling thought took root in my mind: perhaps her actions were steeped in envy. It was as if she was attempting to emulate me, to claim what I had worked so hard to build as her own. The realization felt like a punch to the gut because it was an unsettling betrayal from someone I had once considered a confidante.

When Loyalty Hurts

Strangely enough, my long-term relationship with my boyfriend began to experience its own set of challenges around the same time. It seemed as if the universe had conspired to put me through a trial by fire, testing the very foundations of the connections in my life. The intensity of the situation left me questioning everything...what I held dear, who I could trust, and the nature of loyalty itself. Should I confront her with what the hairdresser said, the one who had inadvertently revealed so much? Or should I listen to my intuition, which warned me that this mess should have never crossed my path in the first place? The cacophony of emotions and uncertainties weighed heavily on my heart, compelling me to pause and assess how I wanted to navigate this tumultuous chapter of my life.

When Loyalty Hurts

I often reminded myself of a saying that echoed in my mind: "What looks like 24-karat gold isn't always gold at all; the eye will fool you every time." This truth rang especially poignant as I navigated the murky waters of friendship and love. Just because something shines brightly at first glance doesn't mean it pure or genuine. It became painfully clear that appearances could be deceiving, masking the deeper currents of jealousy and insecurity that lay beneath.

As I stood at this crossroads, I let the rift grow and fester. While the thought of confrontation filled me with dread, I understood that silence might only prolong the pain. But who was I to dig for truths that perhaps she wasn't ready to reveal? In the midst of this turmoil, I made the difficult decision to cut her off entirely, trusting that my intuition was more accurate than any reassurances she might provide. Deep down, I knew that preserving my own emotional well-being was paramount, and I could no longer afford to remain entangled in a friendship that felt increasingly toxic.

With this internal struggle fresh on my mind, I felt the weight of the situation pressing down on me. I had to decipher whether my intuition was guiding me towards resolution or leading me deeper into a labyrinth of heartbreak. As I prepared to take the next steps in this tangled journey, one thing was becoming increasingly clear: the chapters ahead were bound to challenge everything I thought I knew about loyalty, friendship, and the true nature of love.

"A person who is disloyal is worse than an enemy. At least an enemy doesn't pretend."

-Author Unknown

Chapter 4
Betrayal & Deceit

Approximately a year after the rift in our friendship, the unexpected happened: she reached out. At first, it was subtle messages relayed through mutual friends, accompanied by a text that felt almost like a lifeline, urging me to sit down and talk about the situation. She even had the nerve to send me a text declaring her love for me, expressing a deep desire to reconnect. Yet, something inside me wouldn't let me fall for it. Her words seemed laced with declarations of love and desperate pleas to reconnect, as if time could simply erase the wounds that had festered between us. Beneath her heartfelt messages, I sensed a lingering doubt, a reminder of the hurt that had once driven us apart. But I hesitated because my heart was just too heavy with the memories of betrayal that haunted my mind. I couldn't shake the reluctance that gripped me, an invisible chain tethering my thoughts to the past. Trust had been shattered, splintering into pieces that cut deep, and I knew that opening that door again would risk exposing myself to the same pain I had endured before.

The allure of reconciliation tempted me, whispering nothings of nostalgia. I could picture us traveling together again, laughing as we recounted old stories or planning our next adventure. Yet, lurking beneath that desire was a nagging fear, a reminder of the fragile state of our connection and the scars it left behind. In those moments of reflection, I found myself wrestling with the idea of forgiveness, not just for her, but for myself as well. Could I truly forgive what had happened? Could I allow myself to be vulnerable again? As I weighed the possibility of reopening that chapter, I pictured our past contrasting sharply against the cold reality of our fallout. Would it be naive to

When Loyalty Hurts

believe that we could return to what we once had? Would trusting her again mean risking my emotional well-being?

In the depths of my contemplation, I realized that the journey of healing was complex and unpredictable. I owed it to myself to tread carefully, to assess not just her intentions but my own readiness to delve back into a friendship that had brought so much joy yet harbored such profound hurt. Torn between desire and caution, I was left at a crossroads once more, aware that my next decision could either mend what was broken or reinforce the walls I had built to protect my heart.

Just when I thought the storm had settled, a revelation shattered my fragile reality. The moment she learned of the cracks in my relationship with my boyfriend, the air around us thickened with unspoken tensions. She moved in like a quiet snake, hissing for her prey. I could barely catch my breath as she unleashed a wave of betrayal that turned my world upside down.

She made her move like a predator eagerly pursuing her prey. It was a strike so ruthless it cut deeper than any knife. She went after my boyfriend. The very person I had confided in, the one I believed would stand by me, was now the woman who carried deceitful affection. In that heartbeat, loyalty transformed into a weapon, leaving me reeling in the aftermath of betrayal. My heart raced as I wondered how someone could be so brazenly cruel! I felt the ground shift beneath me.

The realization hit me like a tidal wave, flooding me with emotions I thought I had buried. How could she betray me in such a callous manner? It was as if I had unwittingly handed her a weapon to exploit my vulnerabilities, and in that moment, the lines between friendship and rivalry blurred into a chaotic mess. The trust that had once defined our bond crumbled beneath the weight of her actions, revealing the rawness of my hurt.

When Loyalty Hurts

"It's hard to tell who has your back, from who has it just long enough to stab you in it."

– Nicole Richie

Chapter 5
My Friends & My Man

As I processed the betrayal, a whirlwind of thoughts consumed me. Did she truly think she could effortlessly swoop in and claim my boyfriend? Did she relish in the chaos she had unleashed? It felt like a cruel twist of fate, and I could only wonder if perhaps envy had become her guiding force.

The ache in my chest grew heavier as I faced the reality of the situation. I was left to confront the fact that not only had I lost a friend, but I now stood on the brink of losing the very relationship I had cherished. The balance of loyalty had shifted in ways I hadn't anticipated, and the implications were far-reaching.

As I navigated the emotional fallout, I knew that the ramifications of her actions would force me into a reckoning with both my heart and my choices. It was a tumultuous period of self-reflection and determination...what would I do next? Would I fight for the love I had built, or would I recognize the lesson buried in this pain and reclaim my power? With my world suddenly turned upside down, I realized that reclaiming my narrative would take courage, resilience, and, above all, an unwavering commitment to my own truth.

You may be wondering how I came to learn of this betrayal with my friend and my man...Well, one fateful day, my best friend of over 20 years sent me a picture. Just one photo, one text message, one gut-wrenching betrayal that shattered a lifetime's worth of memories. I was curled up on my couch, phone trembling in my hand, when I opened that message. The image was blurry; his face was obscured, but I recognized that body believe me. I had lived with him, built a life with him, shared my deepest secrets with him. How could I not know him?

But wait it wasn't just him in that photo. His arms were wrapped around someone with a shaggy bushy blonde wig on. It was someone who I once called a friend, the very woman I had distanced myself from. I felt her disloyalty before she even revealed herself, but I didn't know it would be like this. My heart plummeted. How could she betray me like this? I had loved him fiercely for four years. That picture felt like a knife, twisting deeper with every breath.

In an instant, my world crumbled. Where there was once peace and thriving businesses, was now chaos. Lifelong friendships, once cherished, began to unravel before my eyes. I felt the foundation of my life shaking and everything was spiraling out of control. This wasn't just heartbreak; it was the end of the reality I thought I knew oh so well. The unfolding of these events is not merely a tale of heartbreak; rather, it serves as the cornerstone of my journey toward healing and empowerment—a transformation I never anticipated. The betrayal hit like a storm, uprooting everything I thought I knew about loyalty and trust.

As I reflect on those days, I find myself immersed in a whirlwind of emotions, each memory laced with the sting of disbelief. It began subtly, as most betrayals do, masked in the guise of camaraderie and trust. I was surrounded by familiar faces, each smile seeming genuine, each laugh echoing warmth. But beneath that façade lingered a chilling secret; a truth so potent it shattered the very core of my existence. When the revelation came crashing down, it felt as if the ground had given way beneath me. I remember the moment vividly. The cold grip of betrayal wrapping around my heart like a vice. My mind raced; how could the people

I trusted inflict such pain? With every question that surfaced, I grappled with the chaotic emotions swirling within me: anger, sadness, and a profound sense of loss.

Let me tell you, this felt like a scene straight out of a TUBI movie. I couldn't believe that she would stoop so low. Even though we were no longer friends, I never imagined she would go after my man especially after everything we'd been through. Who does that? I thought we had some level of respect for one another, even if we weren't speaking. She knew exactly how I felt about him, but that was the only way she knew how to get my attention.

While my relationship with the man I loved began to unravel, I gradually uncovered the true nature of those around me. It was as if a veil had been lifted, revealing the envy and jealousy that festered beneath their smiles. Women I had trusted, whom I considered my lifelong sisters, turned out to be competitors, each vying for a slice of the happiness that I had created for myself. Their flattering words held a sharp edge, their compliments dripping with hidden disdain.

I can still feel the suffocating moment when my best friend of over 20 years sent me the photo that shattered my reality. It was a snapshot of betrayal, revealing secrets that had been whispered behind my back. I found myself questioning everything: Why didn't she call me first? Hadn't our bond warranted at least a heads-up? Instead, I was struck down by a digital image that plunged me into total shock.

I had everything I thought I needed but hidden beneath every smile and "I love you" was a snake, coiled and ready to strike.

When Loyalty Hurts

Like pieces of a malignant puzzle falling into place, I started to see how each of them played their part. The friend who always seemed enthusiastic about my successes, only to later belittle them in private. The one who, under the guise of concern, would eagerly feed me doubt, subtly diminishing my confidence. And then there was the so-called "sister" who always appeared to support me, yet her eyes would flicker with envy each time I shared my triumphs. All of them were snakes everybody played a role against me!

Together, they formed a coalition of deceit, each one contributing to the web of competition that ensnared me. The reality I had built -the friendships, the laughter, the bond that I thought was unbreakable had been nothing more than a fragile facade, teetering on the brink of collapse as their true motives unfurled. Suddenly, the bonds that had once felt unbreakable seemed like fragile threads ready to snap. But instead

When Loyalty Hurts

of succumbing to despair, I made a conscious choice to rise from the ashes. This betrayal became my catalyst, igniting within me a fierce determination to reclaim my power. I immersed myself in self-discovery, peeling back the layers of hurt to expose the resilient spirit lying beneath. I learned that healing is not a linear path; it is a series of ups and downs, moments of clarity interspersed with shadows of doubt.

The insanity of it all hit me like a freight train; I was blindsided but little did I know that this woman and my so-called best friend were in cahoots together. She used my best friend to deliver a picture to me. The very person who had been calling me, feigning reconciliation, had secretly orchestrated this betrayal. She had told my lifelong friend to send me that picture; it was a premeditated strike, a calculated move that sent my world spiraling into darkness.

When Loyalty Hurts

The shattering realization that my trust had been weaponized sent an icy wave through my veins. What was once a life filled with love and support morphed into a battlefield fraught with betrayal and heartbreak. This was only the beginning of the unraveling, with shadows of deceit lurking behind every corner.

I can hardly wrap my mind around what just happened. My friend, the one who had been reaching out, trying to make amends, sent me something that shattered the little trust I had left. She took something that shouldn't have been shared and sent it to me through another friend of over 20 years, all the while pretending it was a surprise and she just seeing it. But deep down, I knew better. The truth hit me like a cold wave—she and the woman in the picture had become inseparable, best friends, because they both had undercover envy against me reveling in a bond that made them closer. I never knew existed.

When Loyalty Hurts

I saved the picture from the text, my fingers trembling uncontrollably as I zoomed in, my heart pounding in my chest like a war drum. Each detail of the smiling faces sent shockwaves through me, fueling a tempest of emotions that threatened to erupt. I was straddling a fine line between disbelief and rage, dangerously close to crossing over into chaos. There she was...the woman I had once trusted implicitly standing next to him, her arm casually draped over his shoulder, a sinister grin plastered across her face as if she belonged there, as if she had always been the one to share in our moments. In that instant, my heart plummeted, and a cold, hard reality set in. The gut-wrenching realization hit me like a freight train: they had conspired behind my back, plotting and scheming in shadows I couldn't see. I could almost hear the mocking laughter echoing in my ears, taunting me for being blind to the betrayal.

"Stop! Just pause for a moment," I told myself, desperately trying to collect my thoughts amid the whirlwind spiraling out of control. The disbelief tossed me like a rag doll; I could hardly breathe. How could this betrayal come from two people I held dear? Then came the heartbreak, raging and twisting like a feral beast within me, clawing at every shred of joy I had ever felt. Each memory of laughter and shared secrets twisted into daggers that drove deep into my chest.

But it was the anger that ignited a firestorm within me, fierce and unrelenting. I could practically feel it building, surging through my veins like molten lava ready to erupt. The betrayal was a knife to my soul, fueling my rage and compelling me to act. "This isn't just happening to you; this is war!" I thought. I envisioned confronting them, demanding answers, exposing their treachery under the harsh light of truth.

When Loyalty Hurts

"A broken friendship can leave scars deeper than a lover's betrayal,"

Chapter 6
Healing Is A Process

After the devastation of seeing my friend and my man all boo'd up, I had to find myself again even though it took a little while. I delved into new experiences, sought out new relationships, and confronted my emotions head-on. Each step was a testament to my growth, a gradual rebuilding of the trust I once had in myself and in others. Slowly, I began to see that through this pain, I was forging a stronger, more aware version of myself. I emerged from the darkness not merely as a survivor of betrayal but as a warrior claiming her narrative. This journey taught me valuable lessons about loyalty and trust, reminding me that true strength lies in resilience. While the echo of that betrayal still lingers in the background, it no longer defines me. It is merely a chapter in my story

When Loyalty Hurts

and a chapter that empowered me to rise and embrace the beautiful possibilities that life has to offer.

As I share the story of my life, my pain, and the tumultuous journey that has shaped me I hope to shed light on the intricacies of loyalty, friendship, love, betrayal, and the unexpected turns that life can take when your back is against the wall. Each chapter of my life is etched with lessons learned through heartache and moments of clarity that emerged from the depths of despair. It is in these struggles that I discovered the true nature of loyalty, revealing its duality and a powerful bond that can uplift while simultaneously holding the potential for betrayal.

Through my experiences, I have come to understand that friendship can be a fragile thread, easily frayed by misunderstandings and envy. The relationships we cherish are often layered with complexities that can transform love into a battleground where trust is tested and loyalty questioned. Yet, amidst the chaos, there exists an unyielding hope which is the belief that even in the darkest moments, we can find a way to navigate through the pain and emerge stronger.

This wasn't merely a betrayal; it was chaos incarnate, a whirlwind of turmoil that consumed everything I held dear. Gone was the man who once showered me with love and affection; in his place stood someone who believed he was above it all, untouchable bigger than the program that once guided him.

What had once felt like a sanctuary now transformed into a battleground, and I was left grappling with the shards of loyalty that threatened to cut me deep. Every encounter, every moment of intimacy we had shared, now felt like a cruel illusion, overshadowed by this monstrous reality. How did love turn into this suffocating nightmare, where I was no longer his partner but a hostage of his chaos? As the chaos unfolded around me, an icy chill seeped into every corner of my life.

But from the ashes of betrayal, I began to rise. I discovered an inner strength I had never known, the ability to cast aside the toxic relationships that had suffocated me. What I lost was painful, yes, but what I gained was far greater; the clarity to recognize my true worth and the freedom to seek genuine connections, free from envy, jealousy, and competition. My story was no longer defined by their serpentine treachery but by my resilience and the blossoming of authentic relationships grounded in love and trust.

As my relationship with the man, I loved began to unravel, I saw right through his sneaky ways as the layers of his deceit began to peel back. Unfortunately,

When Loyalty Hurts

I found a web of manipulation that ensnared more than just him. My o called "friend" had conspired with women I once considered my lifelong sisters and their disguised envy festered like a hidden wound. They had become the very architects of my betrayal.

I still remember that suffocating moment—the one that felt like the ground had been yanked from beneath my feet when my best friend of over 20 years sent me a photo that shattered my reality. "Why didn't she call me first?" I thought, desperately wishing to brace myself for the impending storm. But there it was, the digital image that plunged me into total shock, a vivid testament to the betrayal I never saw coming.

During my healing process I kept hearing in my mind, "Look at this… this looks like your boyfriend!" Those words punctured my heart. It made my pulse quicken, and I remember an icy grip tightening around my stomach as I scrutinized the picture. In that instant, a horrible realization cascaded over me like a dark wave, and I could barely whisper the words that confirmed my worst fears: "That is him."

The fabric of my world was unraveling right before my eyes, and I was not about to sit back and let it happen. I could imagine myself storming into the room where they reveled in their deceit, confronting them face to face. Would I shatter their perfect little illusion? Would I drag their betrayal into the light, turning their smiles into maskless horror?

With every ounce of determination, I vowed silently that this storm brewing inside of me would not spell my end; it would be my reckoning. Gritting my teeth, I imagined myself rising from the ashes of this betrayal, a phoenix reborn. They may have thought they could take everything from me, but I would reclaim my life, my narrative, and my strength.

No more would I allow myself to be a pawn in their twisted game. This was just the beginning and a spark igniting a fierce resolve to not only confront the storm but to become it. I would unleash my fury, channeling the chaos into a force of empowerment, determined to rise and show them what betrayal truly looks like when I regained control. Healing is a process and it is hard because you have to make the decision to forget and forgive or to remember and be in rage. And I will be honest...there was rage. Internal rage. Many times, I sat stunned in silence thinking back to how I had my phone clutched in my hand while being lost in the dawning realization that the very people I trusted had left me blindsided, conspiring against me the entire time. The room began to spin as anger boiled within me. How could they do this? THE WHOLE TIME! It was nobody but God who was controlling my anger.

Let me take you back to the depths of my friendship with her. When I first introduced this woman to my circle of long-time friends—those who had stood by me for 20 years didn't warm up to her. They saw through her charming facade, but I, blinded by loyalty, insisted she was alright. And so at that moment began a twisted saga, one where envy seeped into the cracks of our relationships. Now, as I observed the snakes bonding over whispered secrets, it became painfully clear: they all coveted what I had.

We were inseparable; she was like a sister. She often slept over at my house, especially during her tumultuous fights with her boyfriend. I became her refuge, a fixture in her life. Through countless late-night talks and tearful moments, I offered my

When Loyalty Hurts

unwavering support. I thought our bond was sacred, forged in the fires of shared struggles and laughter. Yet, here I stood, shattered by the realization that to her, our friendship was as disposable as a passing trend.

Her true quest was for attention and popularity were two things that I never cared about. It was a cruel irony; while I sought genuine connections, she reveled in the glamour of superficial alliances. They say to keep your enemies close, but in this case, I had invited my betrayer into my heart. As I recalled our shared moments, the laughter and love now felt tainted, overshadowed by the betrayal I couldn't yet fully comprehend.

Little did I know that while I was crafting a bond of trust, she was silently plotting her ascent, her ambitious heart blind to the loyalty I extended so freely. She wanted my body, my friends, and my man...everything I held dear just as if my life was just another trophy to adorn her collection of conquests.

As I recalled our shared moments, the laughter and love that once felt genuine now felt tainted, overshadowed by the betrayal I couldn't yet fully comprehend. Every inside joke we had exchanged now felt hollow, filled with shadows of deceit I had yet to uncover. The late-night conversations where we swore we would always have each other's backs transformed into echoes of false promises that rang painfully in my ears.

In a world so enamored with appearances, it was as if our lives had become a twisted game of charades. I had thought we were allies, but she had become an actress playing her role far too well, her eyes gleaming with ambition as she plotted her moves. I was left to question everything...had I been a pawn in her game? Had every smile, every moment of camaraderie been nothing more than a scripted scene in her grand production of life? As the truth unfurled like a dark tempest, I felt the weight of realization settle heavily upon my shoulders. Her betrayal was not merely a personal blow; it was a harsh lesson in the complexities of human desire, a reminder of how easily trust could be manipulated in the pursuit of popularity. In the quiet moments of reflection that followed, I grappled with the stark contrast between my longing for depth and her hunger for validation, searching for clarity in the chaotic maze of emotions that churned within me.

In this tangled web of loyalty and betrayal, the path ahead remained obscured, but I realized that my quest for authenticity was far more worthy than the empty games she played.

When Loyalty Hurts

"Yet each man kills the thing he loves. By each let this be heard: Some do it with a bitter look. Some with a flattering word. The coward does it with a kiss. The brave man with a sword."

-Oscar Wilde

Chapter 7
The Wedding

Brace yourself for the next shocking detail: that woman, the one I once called my friend, married my man. Yes, you heard me right—she did it in a mere 30 days. They tied the knot in 2023...yes, that's right.... while I was left amidst the wreckage of their deceit and my heart in ruins. It felt as though they had orchestrated their betrayal with meticulous precision, waiting for the perfect moment to land the crushing blow that would shatter my heart into a million pieces. In just one month, the person I had trusted with my deepest secrets and vulnerabilities was now plotting to take everything from me. The cruel twist of fate was that she made sure the entire world was watching. Their wedding was splashed across social media, each post a dagger twisting deeper into my wound. Images of their beaming smiles and claimed devotion became a grotesque spectacle, a digital parade of humiliation that felt unbearable.

We went viral, but not for the reasons anyone would celebrate. Instead of joy, I became a tragic figure—a spectacle of heartbreak, an object of pity whispered about at brunch tables and on online threads. My once-close friends watched me unravel, their sympathy laced with the unspoken acknowledgment of what I had lost. Every notification felt like a reminder of my betrayal, as if the universe was conspiring to keep my pain at the forefront of everyone's minds. In the blink of an eye, I had gone from cherished confidante to an unwilling star in a grim reality show...a narrative penned by those I had once held dear. With each passing day, it became painfully clear that every friend I had known for over two decades had turned their backs on me, choosing her over me. Friends I had introduced her to...they were the ones who once called me "Sis" and professed their unwavering love for our bond which had been seduced by her allure. She wielded money like a weapon, knowing full well it could captivate those raised on survival instinct, leaving them oblivious to the true meaning of loyalty. It felt like a betrayal on a scale I never imagined possible, a seismic rupture that shattered my foundation.

As if that wasn't enough, she began to taunt me on social media, a cruel puppet master dancing on the strings of my heartbreak. She posted elaborate photos of their opulent wedding, each image a carefully curated display of extravagance that seemed to mock my pain. The lavishness was something straight out of a fairytale, a million-dollar affair flaunted like a trophy, sparkling with the sheen of unattainable dreams. Meanwhile, I was left behind in the shadows,

When Loyalty Hurts

frantically trying to pick up the fragmented pieces of my shattered life.

With every post, it was as if she was holding a mirror up to my despair, reflecting back a life I had loved—now irreparably tainted. Friends I had once relied on showered her with praise, their comments a chorus of admiration that stung like salt in an open wound. I could only watch in horror as they fawned over the illusion she had created, their words echoing in my mind like a betrayal anthem. It wasn't just my heart that was broken; my entire world was crumbling, and I was left standing in the wreckage, grappling with the haunting realization that loyalty had become a fleeting memory, buried under the weight of greed and deception.

The audacity of it all was astounding. She had the nerve to confront me with a smirk, her eyes dancing with a twisted pleasure. "Are you mad because I married him, or is it because he married me 30 days after you'd been with him for four years and didn't choose you?" Her words slithered through the air, laced with malice, and I felt as if I had been struck by lightning. "Or are you mad I had all your friends at my wedding? That's why I got your man, friends, and workers...don't make me come after your business next."

The sheer gall of her proclamation was mind-blowing, a slap in the face that left me reeling. It was a brutal revelation that exposed the depths of her betrayal. This was not just an act of infidelity; it was an assault on everything I held dear...my friendships, my trust, and my sense of self. As she stood there, relishing in her victory, I couldn't help but reflect on how she had played the role of a concerned friend all along. Showering me with affectionate messages that dripped with false compassion, she had woven a web of deceit so intricate that I had willingly walked into it, blind to her true nature.

I remembered countless moments when she had offered a shoulder to cry on, feigning empathy while secretly calculating her next move. She had listened to my fears, my hopes, and my dreams, only to use that intimate knowledge against me. Every time I confided in her about my relationship, every laugh we shared, and every toast to our friendship felt like ammunition for her betrayal. Each moment was a veneer that concealed her venomous intentions.

Her wedding, a celebration she had flaunted on social media, was a masquerade...all the while shot through with irony. She had invited my friends, turning them into unwitting accomplices in her scheme. I could almost feel their loyalty splintering as they stood there, oblivious to the treachery that had unfolded in the shadows. How could they possibly know that the vibrant celebrations of love were, in reality, a sinister coup against me?

As her words echoed in my mind, I was overwhelmed with a whirlwind of emotions: anger, heartbreak, and initially, a sense of defeat flooded through me. I had invested so much in relationships I thought were built on trust and loyalty. I had counted on these women, believed in them, and defended them against any outside criticism. But here she was, the embodiment of treachery, standing in stark contrast to everything I thought I knew about friendship.

But amidst the storm of her taunts, something began to shift within me. I realized that her attempt to belittle me, to take away what I cherished most, would not define my journey. The sheer audacity of her confidence fueled a fire in my soul. If she thought that gloating would diminish me, she was gravely mistaken. It was time to reclaim the narrative...my narrative.

As I stood there absorbing the impact of her words, a renewed sense of resolve washed over me. I would no longer allow myself to be a victim in this story. I began to envision the friendships I truly valued and the ones I had lost along the way, determining to forge new paths out of this devastation. What she saw as a victory was, in fact, my catalyst for transformation.

No longer would I cling to memories tainted by betrayal. I would rise from the ashes of her deceit, stronger and more self-aware than ever. I would surround myself with people who uplifted me, who celebrated my successes without envy, rather than those who sought to undermine my happiness. This was my chance to emerge from the shadows of false friendships and carve out a life filled with genuine love and loyalty.

And so, as I looked into her mocking eyes from pictures, I prepared to write a different ending to this chapter of my life...one where I would triumph over betrayal, forging bonds of authenticity and strength, rising above the drama of her audacity, and reclaiming my own sense of self-worth. The battle was just beginning, but I knew I was ready to fight for a future that belonged solely to me.

Envy and jealousy were powerful forces, capable of turning even the softest souls into merciless predators. I realized then that she and women like her would go to unimaginable lengths just to step into my shoes, to wear my life like a costume. In that moment, it dawned on me: she hadn't just wanted my boyfriend, she craved my entire existence, and she had succeeded in stealing it. The life I had meticulously built was now a relic, an exhibit displayed for the world to nosily scrutinize. She flaunted my happiness as if it were her prize, basking in the fallout of my heartache. I was left to navigate the emotional labyrinth she had created, battling heartbreak and betrayal while she reveled in the chaos, flourishing at my expense.

And yet, as anger and sadness intertwined within me, I knew one truth remained: betrayal may cut deep, but it also ignites a fierceness that can shatter the darkest depths of despair. It felt like something out of a Tubi movie. It was unbelievable, yet all too real. When the news broke, my phone lit up with notifications, each buzz a reminder of the unraveling chaos around me. Friends, acquaintances, and even strangers inundated me with texts and calls, asking what had happened, how it could've happened. The questions piled up like an avalanche, suffocating in their urgency. Everyone seemed to want an explanation, but it was as if I had been thrust into a whirlpool of shock that left me gasping for breath.

Both of us were well-known in our community, respected figures whose lives intertwined closely with those around us. This only intensified the shock and scrutiny. It felt like our lives had suddenly become a twisted plotline that everyone was discussing behind closed doors. I could sense the whispers, the questions lingering in the air and the piercing glances from those who thought they knew the whole story.

In the midst of this whirlwind, I struggled to articulate my pain. The emotional weight pressed down on me, making it impossible to share the excruciating details of my betrayal in the comments on the social sites—a public forum filled with a mixture of concern and curiosity. I felt exposed, vulnerable, and strangely disconnected from the very community that had once embraced me. I wanted to express my truth, but not in fragmentary snippets scattered across social media. Instead, I decided to take a different route. I would write a book and share my truth in the pages that would ultimately serve as an intimate reflection of my journey. It was an act of empowerment and defiance against a narrative that tried to undermine my experience. Writing became my sanctuary, a space where I could pour out my heart, explore the depths of my feelings, and unravel the complexities of betrayal without the noise of judgment or speculation.

When Loyalty Hurts

"For there to be betrayal, there would have to have been trust first."

-Suzanne Collins

Chapter 8
My Turn On Paper

As I sat down to write, I felt a mixture of trepidation and liberation. Each word I penned allowed me to confront the bitterness and the pain, transforming them from raw emotions into a narrative that spoke to my strength and resilience. I wanted readers to see not just the heartbreak, but also the journey of reclaiming my voice and my vision to rebuild my businesses. This was my chance to turn a painful chapter into an empowering testament of survival and a chance to resonate with others who might have faced similar trials.

In addition to gathering my self-worth back from the shattered fragmented pieces, I can honestly say I know how it feels when you're out here rebuilding your peace, piecing your soul back together, and learning to

When Loyalty Hurts

breathe again without the weight of a man's chaos who you used to love pulling you under. It's like you're no longer explaining yourself, defending yourself, or trying to prove your worth to someone who was committed to misunderstanding you from the start.

I had to let them play their roles. Let them post their forced happiness and fake smiles, showcasing snapshots of laughter that echo hollowly in the silent corners of their lives. They spin their web of illusion, crafting a circus act for the world to see, each performance more extravagant than the last, each laugh a carefully rehearsed note in a melody of deception. They twirl and leap, casting shadows that momentarily brighten the gloom of their own realities.

But just as every show must come to an end, so too will this facade. The clowns will tire, their paint will smudge, and the acrobats will falter. Eventually, the show ends, and all the fakes come to the light. The mask slips, revealing the truth hidden beneath layers of artifice. The audience will slowly start to see what was laying behind the dazzling smiles of the confusion, the exhaustion, and the unrelenting pressure to maintain an image that never felt like home.

If you have ever had a friend to betray such as mine did, just know that she will find herself exactly where you were...not in the audience but center stage, bewildered and drained. In her quest for validation, she will wonder how someone who seemed so charming could cloak such cruelty beneath their enchanting exterior. The whispers of betrayal and the echoes of kindness once spoken will collide, her mind spinning with questions that seem to have no answers. After all, it wasn't just the lies that cut deep...No, it was the betrayal that will sear through her heart.

When Loyalty Hurts

See, when she went behind my back and married my man, stealing the love she never had the right to claim, she will eventually obtain her perfectly orchestrated karma.

As the reality crashes down like a shattered mirror, she will grapple with the painful truth...The one she had long avoided, blinded by the allure of the illusion. It is a bitter awakening, a harsh lesson of loyalty tested. In her heart, she will nurture a flicker of hope that maybe, just maybe, the charade can be undone and the sincerity she craved can be salvaged, only to discover that sometimes, the loyalty we extend to others can become our greatest burden.

Her karma and journey of healing will not be easy, but it will lead her to a new understanding of strength and a realization that true happiness is not found in the applause of a fickle audience but in the authenticity of her own heart. The process became cathartic, giving me the clarity, I needed to confront the tangled web of feelings that betrayal had woven in my mind. It was not merely the act of writing; it was a commitment to healing, to rising above, and to ultimately redefine what loyalty should mean in my life. As I continued to pour my heart onto the pages, I realized that this betrayal would no longer hold power over me; instead, it would serve as the foundation of a new beginning, one crafted from the remnants of broken trust but infused with the promise of growth and renewal.

When Loyalty Hurts

"If you spend your time hoping someone will suffer
the consequences for what they did to your heart,
then you're allowing them to hurt
you a second time in your mind."

- Shannon L. Alder

Chapter 9
Moving from the Reality of It All

The wedding pictures spreaded like wildfire, and with each post, she paraded their whirlwind marriage as if it were a victory over my life. Not only that, all my so called friends of over 20 years **were in the wedding**! And please keep in mind I introduced all of them to her. My friends didn't merely turn their backs they sprinted toward her, as if I never even existed. It was surreal, because on her Facebook page, our pictures were still scattered along the timeline, each laughing moment now overshadowed by her wedding glow next to my ex-man.

It felt like she had bought off all my so-called friends, as they abandoned me to flock to her side. Keep in mind friends for over 20 years if they needed me I was there and here's the kicker: while she was busy

When Loyalty Hurts

showcasing her new life, I was left to grapple with the fallout, picking up the pieces of what was once my reality. I was utterly shocked of how the very woman I introduced to my friends could betray me like this. I was nothing but loyal to her and them. These grown women spent years taunting me on Facebook.

Before the wedding happened, I found myself forced to leave the home I had shared with him. He grew increasingly erratic, kicking in doors just to see what I was up too. I guess trying to make sure that I wasn't doing more than him. I changed the locks, completely unaware of the treachery brewing between him and my so-called friend, who had plans to marry him.

After I moved out, one of my so called friends of over 20 years had the audacity to suggest that I could stay over her house because she had a spare room. She said that I was welcomed to come stay at her house until I decided where I was about to relocate too. But keep in mind I could've stayed with my mom, sister, or brother. Well, I went over there but she should've cleaned that house up and maybe I would've gotten off the couch and went into the spare room. The couch was the only part of the house that was suitable for me.

The nerve of these women was astounding. My mind raced with the thought of escaping Alabama altogether, but I had a luxury boutique to run and a tax company that kept my schedule packed. I couldn't just drop everything and leave, especially at that time in my life. I had investments in an 18-wheeler which included my time and my money. I was at a crossroads and had to make a decision. The reality recap was taunting me and breaking me down. So, I decided to leave. Nothing was going to change unless I made a change. It's like all of a sudden my once-bustling world had fell silent. The phone that used to ring off the hook now lay dormant. What felt like loneliness gradually transformed into a much-needed peace.

After making the decision to relocate, clarity returned as I packed my life into boxes, leaving my hard-earned businesses, my boutique, my tax offices, and that 18-wheeler. Everything I invested in I made a business decision to leave behind.

I made the bold decision to move to another state, fueled by the determination to survive. What seemed like an end was actually a new beginning. As I crossed those state lines, I felt the weight of the world lift from my shoulders. But even in this newfound peace, the buzz of social media swirled. My inbox flooded with concerned messages from those still curious about the unfolding mess. Meanwhile, she still took to social media, seeking attention from me. Claiming I was jealous of her and her new life. The irony of it all was

When Loyalty Hurts

astounding; I was the one left in ruins, yet she was spinning her narrative to paint me as the envious one.

It was clear that she wanted a reaction, desperately trying to provoke me. It was almost as if she thrived on the chaos she created, using my name as fodder for her online spectacle. In the depths of my silence, she poured her energy into writing lengthy posts about me, each one more ludicrous than the last. It felt surreal, watching this unfold from the sidelines, as my so-called friends eagerly chimed in beneath her posts, laughing and showing their envy towards me. As I'm reading the comments I'm saying to myself It really was all kinds of snakes around me.

Their comments, dripping with sarcasm and disdain, were a stark reminder of how quickly loyalty can wane in the face of gossip and perceived rivalry. I took a deep breath, choosing to remain grounded amidst the

When Loyalty Hurts

storm. I refused to lower myself to the idea of engaging in such petty drama felt like a betrayal to everything I had worked for. After all, I'm a businesswoman, a figure of poise and professionalism. Why would I allow myself to be dragged into the cesspool of public spectacle and gossip? I knew that by staying silent, I was choosing dignity over drama. I understood that responding to her provocations would only fuel the fire, giving her exactly what she wanted. Instead, I decided to channel my energy into my work, transforming the hurt and anger into motivation for my business. Every time I felt the urge to respond, I reminded myself of my goals and aspirations. I had fought too hard to build my empire to let someone else's jealousy dim my shine.

When Loyalty Hurts

"Stab the body and it heals, but injure the heart and the wound lasts a lifetime."

-Mineko Iwasaki

Chapter 10
Meeting in the Courtroom

When our paths finally crossed, the confrontation I had anticipated turned into a surreal nightmare. To my utter disbelief, she recorded our exchange without my permission, her sly intent revealing itself in her cold smile. The audacity of her next move took the breath right out of my lungs. She had the nerve to sign a warrant against me. This ignited a legal battle that quickly spiraled into chaos, with each day leaving us deeper in a web of deceit and manufactured drama. Back and forth between court date after court date it was draining me.

While she had a warrant out on me, I had already signed one against him, exposing the twisted reality of our situation. The monster I had glimpsed at the end of our relationship was not a fleeting moment of darkness

When Loyalty Hurts

because it was who he had always been. I realized with a shiver that I had been loyal to all the wrong people, tethering my fate to those who sought to undermine me.

In the courtroom, the atmosphere was electric, chaos buzzing around us like a storm about to unleash its fury. The judge, a formidable woman with a piercing gaze, listened intently, her expression shifting as she learned the backstory of our tangled lives. "You mean to tell me you and her were friends for two or three years, and now you're married to her man of four years? What are you doing standing here?" She couldn't mask her incredulity, and I could sense her growing frustration with the absurdity of it all.

In the courtroom with her was my best friend of 20 years, the one I should've given the title of "my daughter" because she was always on my phone, begging for money as if she was my child, but got the audacity to be in a courtroom against me. How could you snake?

The Judge's skepticism only fueled my resolve, and I felt a flicker of hope igniting within me. "This is a bogus warrant," she declared, her voice steady and strong. "I'm dismissing this case." Her words felt like a beam of sunlight piercing through storm clouds. She turned to my ex, who was visibly seething, and added, "You can stand outside the courtroom and wait. You weren't here to know what I encountered, so why are you standing up here now?"

At that moment, the mask he wore faded, and the chaos he had orchestrated began to crumble. The judge could see him for who he truly was which was a warlock of manipulation and deceit. The act he had maintained in the courtroom fell apart, and I reveled in the realization that the tide was turning in my favor. As his face flushed red, the shade reminiscent of my favorite red bottoms, the judge looked at me, her gaze piercing through the remnants of my heartache.

"You're free to go, Ms. Davis," she announced, solidifying my victory in that tumultuous arena. With my determination coursing through my veins, as a said earlier, I made the decision to leave everything behind. I set my sights on another state, navigating into the unknown. Little did I realize that this leap wasn't the end of my story; it was merely the prologue to a transformative chapter waiting to unfold.

Brethren, I do not count myself to have apprehended; but one thing *I do,* forgetting those things which are behind and reaching forward to those things which are ahead, [14] I press toward the goal for the prize of the upward call of God in Christ Jesus.

Philippians 3: 13-14

Chapter 11
The Move Forward

As soon as I crossed those state lines, an incredible sense of relief washed over me like a cleansing tide that swept away the remnants of what I had endured. I felt the heavy weight of my past that was engulfed with betrayal and heartache lift from my shoulders like a fog finally dissipating under the light of a new day.

Yet, leaving wasn't without its pain. I had invested countless hours and over $100,000 of my own money into my boutique, alongside significant investments in the 18-wheelers I had once purchased...the lifeblood of my entrepreneurial dreams. It shattered my spirit to abandon it all, especially knowing the man I once adored had the audacity to forge my name for those very trucks. He was a harbinger of chaos, trampling across my life as if searching to obliterate not just my possessions but my very essence.

To be honest, battling him or clinging to the past had drained me physically, emotionally, and mentally. I was exhausted by the relentless strife and constant upheaval. So, I chose the path of quiet strength, embracing the winds of change that whispered promises of freedom. With every step away from that life, I reclaimed my peace, ready to redefine my existence on my terms. As I looked ahead, the horizon shimmered with possibilities, and I knew that resilience was my new armor, carrying me forward into a brighter future, unbound and unapologetically me.

Her calculated maneuvers in the court of public opinion forced me into a profound reflection on the twisted dynamics of trust and betrayal that had intertwined our lives. She had coveted my life, and now, in a twisted sense of accomplishment, she believed she had claimed it. Yet, what she failed to grasp was that her reckless invasion into my world came at a heavy cost and one she wasn't prepared to pay. Now, she was bearing witness to the monster lurking beneath the surface, discovering that desperately wanting another woman's life isn't necessarily the fairy tale she imagined.

Behind the mask of her envy lay a stark and unsettling reality she was all too eager to overlook. She was now experiencing the relentless struggle of a life lived in my shadow and the countless late nights I had poured into my dreams, the sacrifices that weighed heavily on my heart, and the challenges I had bravely faced alone. Each setback I encountered had forged my resolve; every obstacle had hammered my spirit into the steel it had become. I had built my success on grit and tenacity, and now she found herself lost in the very chaos she had sought to emulate, drowning in the repercussions of her own decisions.

While she reveled in my name, spinning her fantasies and feeding the insatiable gossip mill with my trials, I transformed my pain into profit. I immersed myself in my passions, pouring my soul into the pursuits that defined me. I rediscovered the solace in my work and was ecstatic about how each task was a small triumph. Each accomplishment was a reminder of my strength. In a world that often clamored for superficial approval, I found true fulfillment blooming from within, resilient and unyielding while being replanted in my newness. Even though I was long gone, her fabrications unraveled and spiraled into ever more absurd narratives, but I stood firm in my conviction. I knew with unwavering certainty that my truth would always shine brighter than the web of lies she spun from her

When Loyalty Hurts

insecurities. With every passing day, I reclaimed my narrative, determined to take back my power and rise above the shadows of betrayal. The darkness she cast could never overshadow the light of my unwavering spirit; loyalty had led me astray, but now, I was armed with the understanding necessary to forge ahead, fiercely, and unapologetically myself.

In the end, I realized that those who truly knew me would see through the fog of her accusations, discern the truth from the tale she spun. I would emerge not only unscathed but stronger, fortified by the knowledge that betrayal reveals character. It reminded me of the importance of surrounding myself with genuine allies, those who uplift rather than tear down. This experience would fuel my ambition, igniting a fire in me that would not be extinguished by anyone's attempts to belittle my journey. I was in control of my narrative, and as I moved forward, I remained steadfast in my commitment to rise above and thrive.

This entire situation unveiled the true colors of everyone I once considered close all at one time. She was trying to take my ego, my life and shred them before the world. On Facebook, she boasted, "That's why I took all your friends and your man." Those words were a sickening reminder of how far she had gone to win this toxic game.

It felt as if they reveled in their attempts to humiliate me. Even though they had orchestrated my downfall, I was not about to drag down another woman's character to lift myself up. Meanwhile, she unleashed a barrage of relentless attacks on my reputation, desperately trying to elevate her status because she was an outsider from a small town called Union Town, Alabama, or somewhere nearby.

When Loyalty Hurts

When I emerged from the courtroom battle victoriously I knew I had to wipe the slate clean and begin fresh. It became my mantra: my past does not define who I am destined to become. I consistently reminded myself that I was a woman first and foremost, before anything else. While my circle once brimmed with 10 to 15 women, I now focused on cultivating relationships with business partners who shared my ambitions, rather than looking for friendships or attention.

I often found myself alone, reflecting during long nights and quiet days. Memories flooded back to the time I slept on my ex-friend's couch during my hardest days, an invitation she extended. The sting of betrayal was profound when one of my adversaries discovered my presence and publicly ridiculed me with a venomous social media post: "You ain't got nothing no more. You at your friend's house sleeping on the

When Loyalty Hurts

couch." Each word hurt like a dagger. How did she know I was at my friend's house, especially when the other friend was the one who had invited me over? So, there it was...another snake had shown her hand. This particular friend was one that I helped if she didn't have anything. Let me be a bit clearer...this is one that I helped if she went to the casino and lost all her money and her baby daddy money too.

The audacity of her to try and belittle me like that. The twisted irony gnawed at me, a bitter reminder of the betrayal lurking beneath her so-called kindness. It felt as though they conspired to revel in my misfortune, quick to gossip and mock as if I were merely a character in their drama. I could almost picture their smug satisfaction at seeing me momentarily broken. But they were fully unaware of my resilience and my innate drive to rise once more. Growing up in a neighborhood where we were taught to rise from any

When Loyalty Hurts

fall, no matter how bruised or battered, had instilled in me an unshakeable spirit. For far too long, I carried a heavy, suffocating shame about how they treated me, about their relentless efforts to tarnish my reputation in the eyes of others. Since you're reading this, let me make one thing crystal clear: the lengths they went to by trying to paint me as delusional was nothing short of pathetic. They went out of their way to steal a man who never deserved my love in the first place, all while pretending to be my friend and quietly plotting my demise. Their actions spoke volumes about their character, about what it meant to be a woman driven by envy rather than empowerment.

At one point, this woman had the audacity to declare her intentions to take over my boutique, planning to rename it from "Elevate Diva" to "The Realest Elevate Diva" or "Elevate Diva 2." Envy at its finest. The venom dripping from her intentions was palpable; I

When Loyalty Hurts

could feel her demonic spirit lurking in the shadows. Ignoring her only fueled her rage, while she relentlessly pursued everything I had poured my heart and soul into. I now understood the truth behind the adage that some people genuinely yearn for your life. I had experienced firsthand how envy can morph into a disturbing reality.

There were times when my chest ached with embarrassment and despair. I isolated myself, shutting out the world, as the thought of facing those who had reveled in my anguish felt unbearable. But one day, amidst that darkness, a flicker of recognition sparked within me. I remembered the fierce, unapologetic woman I used to be and made a solemn vow to shake off the weight of their malice. If they could flaunt their smiles and take selfies while they orchestrated my downfall, then I could certainly reclaim my happiness and rise with dignity.

When Loyalty Hurts

As for him, the one who had contributed significantly to my heartache...he seemed utterly unaffected by the chaos surrounding me. But I refused to stay trapped in a cycle of depression and anger. I began to transform, both inside and out. Without even trying, I had shed the weight that had once burdened me, going from over 200 pounds to a lean 175, and even more. It felt like a resurrection, a reclamation of my self-worth. As Beyoncé wisely said, "the best revenge is your paper." And, as Kash Doll pointed out in her song, '*Kash Kommandments*', "If there are any points to be made don't be scared to prove it and you better look good when you do it.'

The metamorphosis I underwent fueled a fire within me that could not be extinguished. I channeled my energy into my passions and my business and every day I got a step closer to the woman I knew I was destined to become.

When Loyalty Hurts

The journey was not just about weight loss or outward appearances; it was about shedding the layers of hurt and resentment that had clung to me like a second skin. With each step I took, I fortified my resolve, transforming my pain into power and my vulnerability into strength.

This time, I was not just rising from the ashes because I was flying. Every moment became a testament to my fortitude, a reminder that I had the power to reclaim my narrative. As I pushed forward, I felt the weight of their jealousy and malice begin to lift and recognized the eclipse of brilliance with my newfound glow. The best was yet to come, and I was ready to embrace it all! No longer as a victim of their cruelty, but as a force to be reckoned with, unapologetically stepping into my destiny.

When Loyalty Hurts

"Remember not the former things, neither consider the things of old. Behold, I do a new thing; now it springeth forth; do ye not perceive it? I will make a way in the wilderness, and a river in the desert."

Isaiah 43:18-19

Chapter 12
The Days Ahead

The most important lesson I learned during this tumultuous journey is that you are the architect of your own happy ending. Regardless of the battles you face, you have the power to create a future filled with joy. If you don't give up, that happy ending is within reach. Can you feel me on this? These days, I tread carefully with my heart because I've seen firsthand how capable people are of deceit and betrayal. I let it be known from the outset that trust is hard-earned, and I remain vigilant when opening my life to others. The determination to recognize when so-called friends turn into enemies or when significant others become strangers is crucial. Listen to your intuition; it will never misguide you. Through it all, I emerged stronger, more liberated, and ambitious than ever before. As time passed, I transitioned into motivational speaking and poured my energy into expanding my businesses. I even launched a medical carrier service, assisted living programs, a credit consulting business, and invested into the stock market world all while being in another state. I kept myself busy and focused. It was during this period of newfound purpose that I realized it was never really about them; I was only in Alabama because of who I was with, clinging to relationships and people that were never meant to be around me.

I've always been someone who values the people around me, but I learned this hard truth: **If they're not truly for you, they don't deserve to be in your life**. I was doing myself a disservice by holding onto those who did not have my best interests at heart. It's often the ones closest to you, you know those who call you "Sis," "friend," or "boo" those who are capable of the deepest betrayals. They know how to cut you and where to cut you because they have gotten close and studied you. Learn from my book and my experience that you need to let people prove themselves worthy. And also remember that everyone can't be a friend but you might can benefit from each other for a mutual project or business venture. Know the difference.

I dreamed about being betrayed once and it was never by strangers; it was always by those I thought were allies. In the light of day, their smiles seemed genuine, and as bright and inviting as the morning sun. Yet, beneath the surface of their laughter and camaraderie, I sensed an undercurrent of jealousy. It was like a dark shadow lurking just out of sight, patiently waiting for the right moment to strike. Each encounter left me with a lingering feeling of unease, as if I were walking on eggshells, forever cautious and fearful of when the next betrayal might unfold.

When Loyalty Hurts

I became adept at reading the subtle cues the slight tightening of someone's smile, the way their laughter seemed to ring hollow when a success of mine was mentioned. It was a cruel game; one I had not chosen but was nonetheless forced to play. Each glance filled with feigned happiness chipped away at my trust, leaving me feeling isolated and vulnerable in a world that I once thought was safe.

In those quiet moments of reflection, when the noise of the world faded and I was left with my thoughts, I turned to prayer, seeking guidance from God. I found solace in the stillness, a haven away from the betrayal that was gnawing at my spirit. Through my prayers, I began to understand that venting to friends often led nowhere but deeper into a pit of confusion and betrayal, as they too seemed entangled in the same web of deceit. Now that I think back, each conversation left me feeling more disheartened, and I soon recognized that sharing my pain merely opened the door for more misunderstandings.

In my solitude, I forged a profound connection with the divine. My relationship with God became my anchor, the solid ground on which I could stand unshaken amidst the chaos. It was in these intimate conversations with the Creator that I found solace, strength, and a sense of direction that I had long been missing. I poured out my heart in prayer and each word was like a feather in the breeze being carried away into the loving hands of the divine.

During those moments of deep communion, I began to see that God was not just an entity to whom I directed my grievances but a confidant who understood the depth of my struggle. I sought His wisdom, and in return, He gifted me with clarity. In these sacred exchanges, I felt a gentle illumination, a soft nudge guiding me through the shadows that betrayal had cast over my life. It became evident that God was not merely present as an observer but actively involved in my healing journey.

With each prayer, I felt the urgency of my worries dissolve into hope. The weight of betrayal that once pressed down on my chest began to lighten, revealing a path forward filled with possibilities. I learned to navigate my relationships with a newfound discernment, recognizing that authentic connections require not just loyalty but genuine love and respect. As I surrendered my hurt and insecurities to God, I discovered what it meant to truly trust again...not just in others, but in myself and in the divine plan unfolding before me. With every prayer, I reclaimed pieces of my heart, patching them with faith, and realizing that even amidst betrayal, I had the power to rise and flourish.

When Loyalty Hurts

This journey of healing transformed my relationship with loyalty from one of fear to one of strength. I learned that loyalty does not always equate to unwavering support; sometimes, it means setting boundaries and prioritizing my own well-being. Through the eyes of faith, I discovered that even in moments of heartache, there lies an opportunity for growth and self-discovery. In the embrace of the divine, I found a sanctuary. I realized that while betrayal had wounded me, it could not define me. Instead, it became a chapter in my story and a necessary struggle that led me closer to the heart of God. As I turned the pages of my life, I saw that true loyalty begins within and must be anchored in the love and trust I cultivated with the Creator. During this tumultuous time, my mom and sister emerged as vital pillars of support, steadfast in their love and unwavering in their commitment to helping me navigate the stormy waters of betrayal and confusion. They were the anchors I desperately needed, reminding me of my worth and the strength that lay within me. Without their guidance, I feared I might have lost myself completely, adrift in a sea of doubt and despair.

Their encouragement came at a time when my spirit felt frayed, and every wave of betrayal threatened to pull me under. One afternoon, over cups of steaming tea that filled the room with warmth, they introduced me to the idea of a vision board. "It's a simple yet transformative tool," my sister explained, her eyes glinting with enthusiasm. "It will help you visualize your goals and aspirations, a way to reclaim your dreams."

I was intrigued by her compassion and enthusiasm, so I agreed to give it a try. We gathered supplies: corkboard, magazines bursting with vibrant images, scissors, glue, and an inviting chaos of colored markers. As we settled in together, I sensed a flicker of excitement growing within me, something I thought had long been extinguished. With each page I flipped through, I was transported to a world filled with possibilities, where dreams bloomed like wildflowers. As I meticulously selected images and words that inspired me, I felt the weight of my past begin to lift. Each piece I chose was imbued with meaning, a reflection of the aspirations I longed to manifest. Pictures of serene landscapes whispered promises of escape, while powerful affirmations urged me to embrace resilience. It was as if I was piecing together a puzzle of my future, one that spoke to my heart and ignited a sense of purpose.

The process became cathartic; it was more than just gathering images; it was about rediscovering myself amidst the rubble of past betrayals. I vividly remember choosing a picture of a mountain peak. For me it was like a symbol of my desire to rise above challenges. I pinned it to the board with a gentle resolve, and a declaration that my journey was still unfolding, no matter how daunting it seemed. I also found images of people laughing, surrounded by businesses partners, embodying the true essence of connection. With each cut and paste, I felt the warmth of my mother's and sister's unwavering support woven into the fabric of my dreams. Their laughter echoed in the corners of my heart. Each chuckle was a reminder that joy still existed and could be reclaimed. As the vision board began to take shape, I felt like a phoenix rising from the ashes. The vibrant colors and dynamic imagery was breathing life into my ambitions. The act of creating this visual representation of my goals became an intimate dialogue between my past and my future. It was a canvas on which I painted my aspirations and dreams, a tangible reminder that my narrative was far from over.

With my mom and sister beside me, I poured my heart into that board, laughing, reflecting, and sometimes even shedding tears. The room was filled with a sense of magic...Almost like a collective understanding that dreams are nurtured not just in solitude but in the love and encouragement that we share with one another. Each image I selected illuminated a new path, one filled with possibility and hope, reminding me that while betrayal may have darkened my journey, love would always light the way.

Once the board was complete, it stood tall in my bedroom, like a shrine to my newfound determination. Every time I glanced at it, I felt invigorated and inspired. The visual manifesto was urging me to pursue my passions without hesitation. It was more than decoration; it was a daily reminder of who I was and who I could become.

In the months that followed, I found myself taking active steps toward my goals, emboldened by the vision I had created. I began to explore new hobbies, reconnect with genuine people, and even set aside moments to nurture my spirit through meditation and prayer. My relationship with my mom and sister deepened, as we celebrated each small victory together, creating a mosaic of love and support that fortified my resolve.

In this journey, I realized that healing isn't a linear path; it's a series of peaks and valleys. The vision board became a symbol of resilience, a reflection of how loyalty in my family transformed my outlook. I came to understand that trust can be rebuilt, not just in others, but within myself. The love and encouragement of my mom and sister became the foundation upon which I rebuilt my dreams and is a testament to the power of support in the face of adversity. From that point on, I moved forward with a renewed spirit, knowing that while I had faced betrayal, I was also surrounded by loyalty which mattered most. With each day, I emerged stronger and guided not only by my vision but by the love that had carried me through the darkest times which brought me closer and closer to the light.

I was determined to break the cycles of negativity and despair that had plagued me for far too long. Refusing to repeat the mistakes of my past became my mantra, echoing through my thoughts like a rallying cry. I envisioned cultivating relationships rooted in love, mutual respect, and genuine support in an environment where my heart could thrive instead of being stifled by fear and doubt.

When Loyalty Hurts

In my previous attempts to forge connections, I often found myself helping other women with their bills, offering support in any way I could. I thought that altruism would build bridges of friendship and trust. Yet, with each act of kindness, it became increasingly clear that many of them only wanted to see me stumble. That realization hit hard, like a cold splash of water jolting me from a comforting dream. I had poured my heart into relationships that were one-sided and toxic, where my generosity served only to illuminate their insincerity.

It was as if God had intervened, orchestrating a necessary removal from that environment to shield me from the negativity that began to seep into my very soul. Even though they world that I once knew had crumbled around me, the events that took place acted as a catalyst for transformation. In the debris of my shattered expectations lay an opportunity to rebuild my life from the ground up, free from the weight of toxicity that had burdened me for so long.

With each fragment I picked up, I embraced a newfound wisdom that guided my heart as it cautiously navigated through life. I learned to recognize familiar spirits and patterns of behavior that signaled danger. It was like being able to recognize the warning bells sounding off in the recesses of my mind. Trusting my instincts became not just a lesson learned through pain, but a vital shield against future hurt. I approached new encounters with a blend of hope and wariness, understanding that true allies are revealed through actions and not just fleeting words.

This journey taught me the importance of discernment; I was more meticulous in choosing who I allowed into my inner circle. I now recognized the profound impact connections could have on my spirit. Each relationship we build with others have the potential to either uplift us or to drag us down into the depths of despair. That awareness empowered me to surround myself with women who embodied strength and the type of women who celebrated my successes and genuinely wished to see me flourish and they didn't have their hands out or constantly asking me for financial help.

Through this transformation, I came to a painful yet liberating realization: loyalty must be mutual. True allies never abandon you, even in your moments of vulnerability. Gone were the days of giving my loyalty freely to those who didn't deserve it. Instead, I began nurturing friendships bound by trust and respect, that elevated my spirit. I surrounded myself with those who only brought positivity into my life.

But as I forged this new narrative, the specter of past betrayals lingered, whispering reminders of what I had endured. It would be easy to slip back into old habits, to allow fear to dictate my choices. Yet, I was resolute in my path. As I accepted the weight of past betrayals and tucked them away as lessons learned, I opened myself to the possibility of genuine connections.

One evening, as I sat with my new circle of supportive women, laughter filled the air. It was a stark contrast to the tension of previous gatherings, where silent judgments loomed ominously like storm clouds. That night, we shared our stories of struggle and triumph, a tapestry woven from the threads of our experiences. There was an electric energy in the room, fueled by vulnerability and honesty, echoing my newfound belief that loyalty thrives in an environment of openness.

Yet, even amidst this warmth, I remained vigilant. Doubt would occasionally creep in, especially when a familiar face from my past would resurface. "What if they came back to test my resolve?" I'd wonder, battling the remnants of anxiety lodged in my heart. But with every passing day, I grew stronger, honing my instincts and developing a radar for genuine intentions.

The ties I formed were now fortified with trust. I had chosen women who inspired me, who championed my successes, and who held me accountable on days when my resolve faltered. I understood that loyalty isn't merely a badge one wears; it's an active commitment to uplift one another, and an assurance that together, we rise or fall.

Each bond blossomed into a glorious reminder that I had liberated myself from the chains of past betrayals, charting a path toward a brighter future.

When Loyalty Hurts

In the end, I realized that choosing joy, peace, and unwavering support meant embracing the beautiful complexity of relationships while maintaining healthy boundaries. No longer did I allow toxicity to infiltrate my spirit. Instead, I held tightly to the truth that true loyalty feels like home...warm, inviting, and steadfast.

As I continued this journey with my new allies by my side, I blossomed into the woman I was always meant to be, forging ahead with a heart that was stronger, wiser, and, above all, unafraid.

To all the women reading this: I understand the agonizing weight of betrayal. It often comes from those you once considered friends or lovers, the very people you thought would stand by you unconditionally. The pain of watching everything crumble that you've built with love and dedication can

When Loyalty Hurts

feel unbearable, especially when those responsible seem to take pleasure in your misfortune.

But I urge you not to let their actions define you or your worth. In the depths of despair, I found solace in my relationship with God, and I learned that my journey was not just about the pain I experienced, but how I chose to respond to it. If you hold on and keep your faith alive, I assure you that a happy ending is always within reach, waiting for you to claim it.

Remember, you don't owe anyone proof of your worth. This realization blossomed within me like a rare flower breaking through concrete. I understood that engaging in a tit-for-tat game or seeking revenge against those who had wronged me would only tether me to their negativity. Instead, I discovered true strength in my ability to rise above it, transforming my pain into a powerful testament to my character.

When Loyalty Hurts

Life had thrown its share of storms my way, each testing my resolve and threatening to shatter my spirit. Yet, through every trial, I learned one essential lesson: my actions would speak louder than my words. My comeback story would be crafted in struggle and perseverance which was more than just my narrative; it became a beacon of hope for others navigating their own tumultuous seas.

It resonated far beyond my experiences, echoing in the hearts of those who felt overwhelmed by their circumstances, reminding them that transformation is indeed possible. As I reclaimed my narrative, I found peace in the aftermath of chaos. This sense of tranquility served as a stark reminder to those who had sought to undermine me. They would watch, and they would witness my rise into a beautiful evolution from the shadows they had casted. I stood tall, not just as a survivor, but as a testament to resilience and grace.

When Loyalty Hurts

Every setback became an opportunity for growth and every whisper of doubt turned into a resounding chorus of self-affirmation.

My journey from darkness into light illuminated the path for others who often felt lost and alone in their battles. I began to share my story, not from a place of bitterness but from a deep sense of empowerment. With each word spoken, I infused my experiences with lessons learned. Women gathered around me, drawn by the authenticity of my message, and together, we formed a circle of support that thrived on encouragement rather than competition.

In these hallowed spaces, we shared our stories each thread woven together with compassion and understanding. The very act of vocalizing our struggles was liberating. I found strength in vulnerability, and with every confession, I saw others' eyes light up with recognition. My words became a balm for their wounds, reminding us all that we were not alone.

As I reclaimed my life, I recognized that my peace wasn't just for me; it was a shared refuge. It became a catalyst for transformation that fueled a community of women who were determined to lift each other up rather than tear one another down. With every exchange of laughter and every moment of solidarity, we cultivated an environment filled with the power of loyalty and not the blind sort that held us captive, but a loyalty born from trust and mutual respect.
And so, my rise became more than just an individual journey; it blossomed into a movement. A circle of women committed to celebrating each other's victories, no matter how small. It was in these moments that I truly understood the importance of surrounding myself with those who uplifted my spirit

and reflected back the very essence of resilience I was striving to embody.

As I faced each new day, I stood confident and unapologetic. For I had weathered the tempest, and with every step forward, I left behind the weight of past betrayals. I embraced my story, my journey as an evolving masterpiece. And I knew, without a doubt, that the power of rising above was not just my strength...it was the shared strength of every woman who dared to reclaim her peace and purpose. Your peace will serve as a stark reminder to those who tried to shatter your spirit. Let them witness your rise; let them see how you've reclaimed your life and your narrative. You've weathered the storm, and now you stand tall because it is your personal and powerful testament to resilience and grace.

My pain was turned to profit.

-Tandreka Davis

About the Author

Tandreka Davis is a passionate storyteller, speaker, and advocate for resilience and empowerment. With a unique journey marked by struggles and triumphs, Tandreka has transformed pain into purpose, using her life experiences to inspire others to rise above life's challenges and reclaim their narratives. In her writing, Tandreka explores themes of loyalty, self-discovery, and personal growth, connecting with anyone who has faced betrayal or hardship. Through her words, she invites readers to embrace their own power and believe that they, too, can craft their beautiful endings. When she isn't writing, Tandreka enjoys reading, traveling, or spending time with family and she actively engages with her community, aiming to uplift and support those on their journeys of renewal.

To book Tandreka Davis for speaking engagements, or to connect with her visit: Elevatedivacreation.com or **Tan Davis** on Facebook where she shares insights, inspiration, and updates on her upcoming projects. Join her on this journey of hope and transformation.

Journal Your Thoughts

This time, you hold the pen in your hand, and you are the architect of your own narrative. Embrace the extraordinary power you possess to craft a beautiful ending. The type that not only reflects your struggles but also celebrates the triumphs that lie ahead. Your journey is uniquely yours, rich with lessons learned and wisdom gained along the way. With each stroke of the pen, you weave together a tapestry that brings you closer to the life you've always envisioned, where loyalty nurtures rather than betrays and where love uplifts instead of harms.

As you continue to write your story, remember this: Every chapter contributes to the masterpiece of your life. Take the time to celebrate your victories, no matter how small they may seem, and learn from your setbacks. Each experience adds depth and richness to your narrative, painting a vivid portrait of resilience. Most importantly, take pride in how far you've come.
The pages that follow are not mere words on paper; they represent your evolution, your growth. Your narrative has the power to inspire others, serving as a guiding

light for those who seek their own renewal amid chaos and confusion. You have the ability to show them that rising above betrayal is possible and that it is indeed within their reach to walk boldly toward their destinies. Let your story blaze a trail for those who find themselves lost in a world filled with betrayal, jealousy, and pain. Your journey can become a beacon of hope, illuminating the path for those in darkness. You will show them that even in the face of adversity, there is strength to be found and they too have the strength to rise, rewrite, and reclaim the narrative of their lives. The ending you create is not merely an end; it is a glorious new beginning. It is an invitation for others to join you on the journey of healing and strength, a testament to the indomitable spirit that resides within each of us. So now, gather your thoughts and go forth with courage.

Write your beautiful ending with conviction and passion. Share your truth with the world, for it is in your authenticity that others will find their own. With every word, you have the power to uplift, inspire, and ignite change, crafting not just a story but a legacy of resilience and hope. Now is the time to embrace your journey fully, grip your pen like a sword, and create the life story you was always destined to tell. The world is waiting for your truth so let it be heard and felt, illuminating hearts along the way.

-Tandreka

This is my story...

When Loyalty Hurts

When Loyalty Hurts

When Loyalty Hurts

When Loyalty Hurts

When Loyalty Hurts

When Loyalty Hurts

When Loyalty Hurts

When Loyalty Hurts

When Loyalty Hurts

When Loyalty Hurts

When Loyalty Hurts

When Loyalty Hurts

When Loyalty Hurts

When Loyalty Hurts

When Loyalty Hurts

When Loyalty Hurts

When Loyalty Hurts

When Loyalty Hurts

When Loyalty Hurts

When Loyalty Hurts

When Loyalty Hurts

When Loyalty Hurts

When Loyalty Hurts

When Loyalty Hurts

When Loyalty Hurts

When Loyalty Hurts

When Loyalty Hurts

When Loyalty Hurts

When Loyalty Hurts

When Loyalty Hurts

When Loyalty Hurts

When Loyalty Hurts

www.ingramcontent.com/pod-product-compliance
Lightning Source LLC
Chambersburg PA
CBHW051941160426
43198CB00013B/2247